LIVING IN THE PAST

TUDOR TIMES

HAYDN MIDDLETON

Series editor: Haydn Middleton

Illustrated by Joan Gammans

Basil Blackwell

INTRODUCTION

This book is part of a junior series on British history. It presents absorbing material on the Tudors, and aims to show the reader that all history is based on *evidence*.

The written sources have been chosen for their vividness and accessibility. In some cases the extracts have been modified to make them simpler for the young reader. All the written evidence is printed in italics throughout the book to distinguish it from the narrative.

The pictorial sources are intended to stimulate close observation and interest. There are follow-up exercises on each double-page spread to encourage the reader to think about the evidence and to develop the important skills of observation, deduction and imaginative reconstruction.

Each book in the series contains double-page spreads on the following topics: Growing Up, Homes, Food and Drink, Clothes and Entertainments. These spreads are identified by recurring symbols, on the pages and in the contents list below. Readers who are doing a project on, for example, Entertainments Through The Ages, can find lots of material by looking at the relevant pages in all the books in the series. Finally, in the section on 'HOW TO BE A HISTORIAN', on page 48, there are suggestions for more investigative project work.

This book is for Nan

CONTENTS

In this book, you will find out a lot about how people lived in Tudor Times. But as you read, keep on asking yourself 'How does the writer know this? How does he know that?' His information about Tudor Times comes from things from those days that are still with us today. They might be paintings, books, letters or even objects like shoes or helmets. *All* these things help us to work out how life used to be — and in many ways it was very different from life today! The list below shows you what you can find out about in this book. Each of the first five chapters is written around different types of Tudor things — these are in brackets in the list. When you have read the whole book, you should be able to say what things have helped him to write *all* the stories.

1 THE SHIP THAT SANK

Picture 1 The 'Mary Rose' sinks!

It was 19 July 1545. England was at war with France. The French king had sent out a navy to invade England. It had to be stopped. The English navy sailed out of Portsmouth harbour. King Henry VIII was watching from the shore, on horse-back. He looked proudly at the *Mary Rose*. It was one of his biggest and best battleships. Then suddenly a terrible thing happened. The great *Mary Rose* began to sink!

No-one was sure why this happened. Perhaps there were too many soldiers and sailors on board. But the ship just kept on sinking. You can see the masts in Picture 1. A man on one of them is shouting for help. Men in rowing-boats are pulling people out of the water. Meanwhile, the battle with the French was beginning.

The English won the battle. But the *Mary Rose* sank to the bottom of the sea. About 600 men were drowned. King Henry VIII was very sad indeed.

Hundreds of years went by. People forgot that the *Mary Rose* was lying on the seabed. It was covered up by mud and slime. This protected lots of the things on board. It stopped them from rotting away to nothing.

4

Not very long ago, some people found out where the *Mary Rose* was. They dived down to the seabed, and they found lots of interesting things. There were skeletons of sailors and soldiers. Some of them still had leather jackets and shoes on. There were great cannons, with cannonballs and gunpowder inside. There were musical instruments, wooden hair combs in leather cases, bows and arrows, candlesticks and stones from plums. There was even the skeleton of a black rat. These rats carried fleas which gave people the plague!

The divers brought up lots of these things. They were cleaned and mended.

Picture 2a

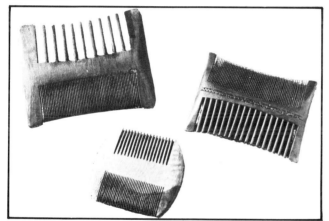

Picture 2b

Picture 2c

Then they were put in a special museum in Portsmouth. Now we can all go and look at them. They help us to find out how people lived, hundreds of years ago. They tell us what people ate, what they wore, what weapons they used and lots more.

In this book, you will see more photographs of things from the *Mary Rose*. You will also learn of other ways to find out about the past. This book is all about England in the years between 1485 and 1603. We call these years TUDOR TIMES. Turn over, and find out why.

✩✩✩ **TO DO** ✩✩✩

1. Pretend you are the man on the mast in Picture 1. Write a letter home, describing what happened on 19 July 1545. Mention: the French navy; King Henry VIII; what people said and did as the *Mary Rose* sank; what you saw in the water as the ship sank.

2. The things shown in Picture 2 were all found on the *Mary Rose*. Name as many of them as you can.

5

2 OFF TO SEE THE KING!

It was 22 August 1485. Two armies were fighting at Bosworth Field in Leicestershire, right in the middle of England. King Richard III led one of the armies. A nobleman called Henry Tudor led the other. Henry's army won. Richard III was killed and Henry became King Henry VII.

In those days, news spread very slowly. But people all over England heard stories about the battle. They wondered what the new king was like. Was he young or old? Was he tall or short, fat or thin, ugly or handsome? King Henry decided to *show* them. He planned to make a tour of his kingdom. This tour was called a 'royal progress'.

He left his palace in London, and visited the cities of York, Gloucester, Hereford, Worcester and Bristol. In each city, there were plays and parties in the streets. People flocked to see the King. On the country roads between the cities, more crowds gathered. They waited to glimpse Henry and cheer as he rode by.

Henry went on lots more progresses around England. He wanted his people to know him and like him. Then they would obey his orders without grumbling too much!

As he travelled around, he kept a note of the things he paid people for. Today we can read these notes. They help us to know what it was like on a royal progress:

Beer drunken at the farmer's house − 1 shilling . . .
to poor women for cherries and strawberries − 1 shilling and 8 pence . . .
to a poor man that had his corn eaten by the King's deer beside Woking − 3 shillings and 4 pence . . .
for a red rose − 2 shillings . . .

Picture 1 King Henry VII on a 'royal progress'

Picture 2   What did Henry VII look like? Someone painted this picture of him in 1505. His wife, Elizabeth of York, had died, and he now wanted to marry a foreign princess called Margaret. So he sent this painting of himself to her. The painter made Henry look a bit more handsome than he really was. Henry hoped Margaret would like the painting, and agree to marry him. But she did not!

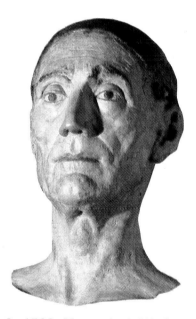

Picture 3   In 1509, Henry died. We know what he looked like then, because someone made this model of his dead face. Also, a man called Polydore Vergil wrote this description of Henry just before he died: *'small, blue eyes; only a few poor blackish teeth; thin, white hair and a pale face.'*

Picture 4   This lock was always used for the King's bed chamber. When the King moved from house to house on his royal progresses, he took this lock with him.

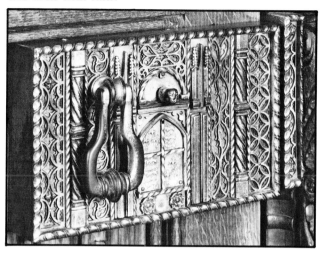

Henry VII was the first king of England from the Tudor family. Two more kings and two queens from the same family ruled England after him. That is why we call the years from 1485 to 1603 TUDOR TIMES.

☆ ☆ ☆ **TO DO** ☆ ☆ ☆

1.   a) Look in an atlas and find the places that Henry VII visited on his first royal progress.

b) Work out a route that he might have taken. Then trace the map and draw in the route.

c) Why do you think Tudor rulers took the lock in Picture 4 with them on progresses?

d) Look at Picture 2 and name one of the things in it which Henry paid for on a progress.

2. Look at Pictures 2 and 3. Which one do you think Henry really looked like? Say why.

7

3 OFF WITH HER HEAD!

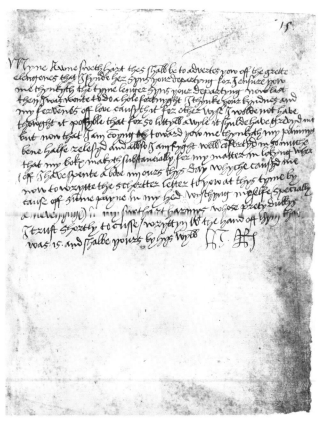

Picture 1

Henry VIII wrote the letter in Picture 1 in 1528. Henry VIII was the son of Henry VII. He was king of England from 1509.

Look at the words in the letter. Lots of them are different from the words we use today. Lots of the spellings are different too. The letter begins '*My own sweetheart*'. Then Henry tells his sweetheart that he is very lonely without her. At the end, he says he is looking forward to kissing her soon! Henry hardly ever wrote letters. So he must have liked this lady very much.

The lady's name was Anne Boleyn. Henry liked her better than his wife, Queen Katherine. He was angry with the Queen, because she had not had any sons. He wanted a son very badly, to take over as king after he died. But the Queen only had a girl, called Princess Mary. Henry thought that a woman would not be able to rule England properly. In the end, Henry decided to divorce poor Queen Katherine. In 1533, he married Anne, because he thought she would have a son.

Later that year, she was crowned queen. Then she had a baby. Everyone prayed that it would be a boy. But it was another girl. Henry was furious. He refused to go to the baby's christening. The girl was called Princess Elizabeth.

Anne had more babies, but they all died. Soon Henry wished he had never married her. Some people thought Anne was a witch, because she had six fingers on one hand. Henry agreed with them. He said that Anne had cast a spell on him, to get him to marry her!

In 1536 she was condemned to death, even though she had done nothing wrong. On 19 May, in the Tower of London, a swordsman cut off her head.

Picture 2a Queen Katherine   Picture 2b Queen Anne   Picture 2c Queen Jane

Henry did not watch Anne die. He was at Hampton Court, playing tennis. Messengers raced there to tell him that Anne was dead. At once he went to see his new sweetheart, Jane Seymour. Very soon, she became his third wife. Henry had three more wives before he died in 1547.

But Henry's daughter, Princess Elizabeth, lived on. One day, she would become Queen of England. She would be an even greater ruler than her father (see pages 42-3).

Picture 3 King Henry VIII

✩✩✩ TO DO ✩✩✩

1. Pretend you are King Henry VIII and write a short letter to Anne Boleyn. Begin with 'My own sweetheart'. Then tell her how much you miss her. You can also pay her compliments on the way she looks (look at Picture 2 first).

2. Describe what the three queens are wearing on their heads and around their necks in Picture 2. In what ways are they dressed differently from modern women? Do you think they would have liked women's fashions today? Say why or why not.

3. Say what sort of man you think Henry VIII was. Do you think he was patient, kind, lively or what? What sort of mood do you think he was in, in Picture 3?

4 AT THE PALACE

Picture 1

Just after Henry VIII died, someone drew this picture. It shows Hampton Court, one of the King's palaces. To begin with, it belonged to a very rich man called Thomas Wolsey. Wolsey was only a butcher's son from Ipswich, but he had become the most important man in the country after the King. He gave Hampton Court to Henry as a present.

Hampton Court is just outside London. London was the capital city of England.

Picture 2 Inside Hampton Court palace today

Henry had to spend a lot of time there. But the city was very dirty and full of diseases. So Henry liked to get away to the fresh air at Hampton Court. There is a story that Wolsey 'asked the cleverest doctors in England, and even some from Padua in Italy, to choose the most healthy spot within 20 miles of London.' They chose the land where Hampton Court now stands. That is why Wolsey decided to build it there. Henry travelled to the palace by barge on the River Thames. You can see the wide river in Picture 1.

Hampton Court palace is still there today. Anyone can visit it, and look at all the beautiful gardens and buildings. Some rooms are nearly the same as they were in Henry VIII's time. As you walk around, you can pretend that you are one of Henry's noble guests.

You would have your own bedroom. There would also be places for your servants to sleep. Sometimes there were about a thousand people staying at the palace! Every day, you would go to services in the Chapel Royal. You could enjoy yourself playing indoor tennis, jousting in the 'tiltyard', or watching plays in the Great Hall. And there was always plenty of ale (beer) to drink. Even a maid of honour was given a gallon for breakfast, a gallon for dinner, half a gallon in the afternoon and half a gallon at supper!

Some days, you might not see the King at all. He would be in his Privy Chamber, having meetings with his ministers. Soldiers stood on guard outside. Sometimes you had to wait for hours before the King could talk to you. But on other days, he joined in all the fun and games at court. He was '*extremely fond of tennis*', wrote an Italian visitor. '*It is the prettiest thing in the world to see him play, his fair skin glowing through his fine shirt.*'

✡ ✡ ✡ **TO DO** ✡ ✡ ✡

1. Make a list of all the things which the royal family does today. How do you think they enjoy themselves at Buckingham Palace? Do you think Henry VIII had a better time than them? Say why.

2. Copy Picture 2 and then draw in a servant, a soldier and a nobleman. Write underneath each person what he is doing.

Picture 3   Dinner for Henry VIII and his guests in the Great Hall, Hampton Court palace. In the smaller picture, you can see the Great Hall today.

5 MONASTERIES IN RUINS

Picture 1

Picture 2

Look at Picture 1. It shows the ruins of Fountains Abbey in Yorkshire today. Until the reign of Henry VIII, monks used to live there. You can read all about monks and nuns in *The Middle Ages*. Picture 2 shows what Fountains Abbey looked like then. Why did the monks stop living and praying there? And why are so many stones and tiles missing from the buildings? Read on and find out.

Until the middle of Henry VIII's reign, everyone in England was supposed to be a Roman Catholic. Everyone had to obey the Pope's religious rules − even the King. But then Pope Clement VII tried to stop Henry from divorcing Queen Katherine (see page 8). This made Henry very angry. He divorced Katherine anyway, and decided that no-one in his kingdom should obey the Pope any

more. He made himself 'Head of the Church' instead.

Henry now made his own religious rules. He closed the monasteries, nunneries and friaries, and seized the fine things inside them and the land that they stood on.

By 1540, all 825 monasteries had been shut down. Nearly 10 000 monks, nuns and friars were told to get out. They had to go and live with their relatives, or take up jobs, or just become beggars. Henry did not feel very sorry for these people. He said that most of them had not been living holy lives anyway.

Henry soon sold lots of the old monasteries and their lands. Rich men turned the buildings into grand houses. Do you know any houses called 'priory' or 'grange' or 'abbey' today? They probably

Picture 3   Hugh Faringdon was the Abbot of Reading Abbey. He was a friend of the King, but he would not hand over his Abbey to him. Henry seized the Abbey anyway, and put his friend on trial. Hugh was called a traitor and condemned to death. He was executed in front of the Abbey gate in 1539.

used to be monasteries. Some old monasteries were just left empty. People came and stole their stone and tiles. They used them to make new buildings of their own. The winds and rain wore away the bits that were left. That is why Fountains Abbey is in ruins today.

Some Tudor people were sad to see the ruins all over the kingdom. They sang:

Level, level with the ground
The towers do lie,
Which with their golden, glittering tops
Pierced once to the sky.

☆ ☆ ☆ ☆ ☆ ☆ ☆ ☆ **TO DO** ☆ ☆ ☆ ☆ ☆ ☆ ☆ ☆

1. Make up a second verse to the song above. Begin with:

Monks and nuns have gone away. . .

2. Henry VIII sent out men to seize precious holy things for him. In 1537, one of them wrote this in a letter from Caversham, near Reading:

I have pulled down the statue of Mary at Caversham. Pilgrims often used to go to it. I have locked it up in a chest. It shall be brought to your Lordship on the next barge from Reading to London. I have also pulled down the place she stood in, with all the lights, crosses and pictures.

Pretend you lived in Caversham, and watched the King's man doing all this. Describe what he did, and say if you thought it was a good thing or a bad thing. What did the other people watching think?

6 THE SCHOOLBOY KING

Picture 1   William Scrots painted this odd picture of Prince Edward in 1546. Close your right eye, and hold the right-hand side of the picture close to your left eye. Then you can see the face properly.

Picture 2   Edward wrote this in French when he was 12. It is part of an essay about religion. Edward's teacher has corrected some of the mistakes.

Picture 3 This is how Edward signed his name, it is from a letter to his step-mother, Queen Catherine. She was Henry VIII's sixth wife.

It was 12 October 1537. Everyone at Hampton Court was overjoyed. Queen Jane had just had a baby boy. At last Henry VIII had a son! The new prince was called Edward. People said he was 'His Majesty's most noble jewel'.

In 1547, Henry died. Edward became King Edward VI, but he was only 9 years old. So first the Duke of Somerset, and then the Duke of Northumberland ruled his kingdom for him. Meanwhile, the young king had to get on with his schoolwork!

Edward was very good at his lessons. He knew Latin, Greek and French as well as English, and he was very keen on music and astronomy (studying the stars). He was especially interested in religion. The Bishop of Gloucester wrote that:

he takes notes of every sermon that he

hears. Then he asks the boys who study with him to discuss these sermons after dinner.

Everyone hoped that Edward would grow up to be a great king. But in 1553 he fell badly ill. In May, a royal servant wrote that:

he does not sleep unless he is stuffed with drugs. His feet are swollen all over. The doctors think he will die within three months.

On 6 July, Edward said a prayer that he had made up himself, and then he died. He was only 15 years old.

Picture 4 A five-shilling piece (5s)
A two-shilling and sixpence piece (2s 6d)
A shilling (1s)
A sixpence piece (6d)
A penny (1d)
A halfpenny (½d)

When the people heard the news, they were shocked. Some of them said that Edward was not really dead. They believed that he had gone to Europe or Africa, and, one day, he would come back and reign in England. Nearly 30 years later, a man was put on trial in Essex. He said that Edward had sailed to Germany in a red cloak, and that there was just a piece of lead in Edward's grave. But the man was wrong. The Schoolboy King really was dead. No more Tudor kings would ever rule England.

☆☆☆ TO DO ☆☆☆

1. The coins in Picture 4 were made in Edward VI's reign. In Tudor times, people used pennies, shillings and pounds. There were 12 pennies in a shilling, and 20 shillings in a pound. People kept on using money like this until 1971. Then they started using the money that we have today.
a) How do we know that these coins were made when Edward was king?
b) How many pennies were there in a pound?
c) What was left if you took 7 pennies away from two shillings and sixpence?

2. What sort of boy do you think Edward VI was? Would you have liked him as a friend? Say why or why not. Would you have liked him as your king? Say why or why not.

7 TWO FAMOUS BOOKS

Pretend that you cannot read or write. Just think what life would be like. You would not enjoy books and comics. You would not understand signposts or notices or instructions. You would not write letters. You would not even be able to sign your own name!

Yet in Tudor times, lots of people *never* learned to read or write. In Norwich in 1600, only 15 labourers out of every hundred could write their names. People who *could* read had to read things out loud to the rest. Very often, they were asked to read bits out from the Bible.

In Roman Catholic countries, the Bible was in Latin. Henry VIII stopped England from being a Roman Catholic country (see page 12). He ordered that the Bible should be in English. Then his people would be able to understand it better.

Picture 1 shows the first page of the English Bible of 1539. Every church had to have one. Look at the top of the picture. You can see Henry handing out Bibles to two important men. On the right is Thomas Cromwell, his chief adviser. On the left is Thomas Cranmer, the Archbishop of Canterbury.

Cranmer was still Archbishop of Canterbury in Edward VI's reign. When Edward died in 1553, his half-sister, Mary, became queen. She decided that England should become Roman Catholic again. Once more, the Pope became Head of the English Church. Some people were very unhappy about this. They were called 'Protestants'. Archbishop Cranmer was one of them.

Mary did not listen to the complaints of the Protestants. Instead she burned nearly 300 of them at the stake. Even Cranmer was put to death. But in 1558, Mary died. Her half-sister Elizabeth became queen, and she was a Protestant.

Picture 1

16

Picture 2

So once again, England stopped being a Roman Catholic country. Ever since then, it has been a Protestant country. (You can find out more about Catholics and Protestants on page 21.)

Elizabeth ordered that another book be put in every church. People called it 'Foxe's Book of Martyrs'. It described how Catholics were cruel to Protestants all over Europe. It was not a very fair book, because it did not show how Protestants were cruel to Catholics too. But many people enjoyed hearing the stories about the 'wicked' Catholics. Picture 2 is from the book. It shows Thomas Cranmer at the stake. 'Foxe's Book of Martyrs' made lots of English people hate Catholics for a very long time.

✰✰✰✰✰✰✰✰ TO DO ✰✰✰✰✰✰✰✰

1. Look hard at Picture 2.

a) Where was Cranmer put to death?

b) What is Cranmer saying? (**Clue** — in Tudor times, 's' was sometimes written as 'f'.)

2. Write down all the things you did last weekend. Which of the things could you not have done if you could not read or write?

3. Fill in the rest of this table for *all* the Tudor kings and queens:

Name	Dates of Reign	Religion of England
Henry VII	1485 to 1509	Roman Catholic

17

8 KILL THE WITCHES!

Picture 1 Some people thought that witches gathered at midnight meetings, or 'Sabbaths'. This painting is from 1607. It shows what witches were supposed to do at Sabbaths.

Have you ever had an accident? Do things sometimes seem to go all wrong? If so, you probably say 'I've been very unlucky.' In Tudor times, it was not like that at all. Most people believed that wicked women *made* things go wrong. They called these women 'witches'.

Men wrote lots of leaflets about witches and their crimes. This story comes from a leaflet of 1585:

Margaret Harkett, of Stanmore in Middlesex, was a widow about 60 years old. She came to William Goodwin's house to ask for some oatmeal. The servants would give her none. Then at once one of Goodwin's lambs, which was in the room with the witch, fell down and died . . .

She came to John Frynde, and offered to sell him a pair of shoes. Her price was tenpence, and he offered her sixpence and would give her no more. This annoyed her, because at that time she had need of money. Then Frynde went to gather pears from off the tree. Suddenly he fell down to the ground. He hurt himself so badly that he could not leave his house . . .

Not long afterwards, Frynde died of a terrible illness. Just before he died, he swore that Margaret Harkett had put an evil spell on him. The woman was put on trial. No-one could *prove* that she was a witch. But she was still condemned to death and killed.

Some people thought witches made secret agreements with the Devil. Then the Devil sent them evil spirits, to help them to do bad things. These spirits were called 'familiars'. They sometimes disguised themselves as cats, dogs, rats, toads, wasps or butterflies. If people saw one of these creatures near a woman, they thought she might be a witch. But to make sure that she was a witch, she was 'tested'. Picture 2 shows two ways that this was done.

Hundreds of women were blamed for accidents and illnesses, and put to death. They were often poor old widows like Margaret Harkett, who had no-one to stand up for them. So it was easy to pick on them.

☆ ☆ ☆ TO DO ☆ ☆ ☆

1. Describe in your own words all the things that are going on in Picture 1. Look hard for: familiars; casting spells; flying on broomsticks. Say how old you think each woman is.

2. Why do you think the leaflet about Margaret Harkett was written? Why do you think the writer wanted people to know about her?

3. Pretend you are a witch being 'tested'. Stand up in front of the class and say the Lord's Prayer. *Remember*: if you make one tiny mistake, the class will condemn you to death! (Boys can do this too. Male 'witches' were put on trial as well as women.)

Picture 2   Testing witches. Below left: If the girl in the chair sinks, she is supposed to be innocent. If she floats, she is supposed to be guilty, because the Devil is helping her. Below right: The old woman is saying the Lord's Prayer. If she does not get it all exactly right, she is supposed to be guilty, because the Devil is stopping her from saying it properly.

9 IN AND OUT OF CHURCH

Do you go to church? In Tudor times you *had* to go once a month at least. If you did not, you had to pay a fine. There were people called churchwardens who kept lists of people who were absent. Picture 1 shows a list from Stratford-on-Avon in 1592. The third name is 'John Shakespeare'. He was the father of William Shakespeare, the great writer (*see* pages 40-41).

Special church courts punished you for working on Sundays or Saints' Days. They also punished you if you misbehaved during services. People were sent to the court for nudging their neighbours, spitting, knitting, making rude comments, telling jokes, falling asleep and even letting off guns!

Some people were very serious about religion. They were called 'Puritans'. They prayed at home, as well as in church. If they could read, they read the Bible over and over. They liked nothing better than a good sermon. Once, a preacher spoke for two hours. When he told the congregation that he would stop, the people shouted back '*for God's sake, Sir, pray go on, go on!*'

Many people had strange ideas about religion. They thought that it was like magic. In 1543, there was a bad storm in Canterbury. The local people ran to the church to get holy water. Then they sprinkled it in their houses. They believed this would drive away the evil spirits in the air, and stop their houses from being struck by lightning!

Picture 1

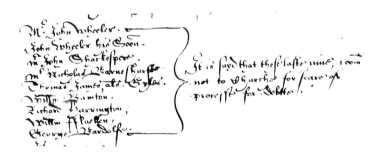

Picture 2　A Tudor church in York

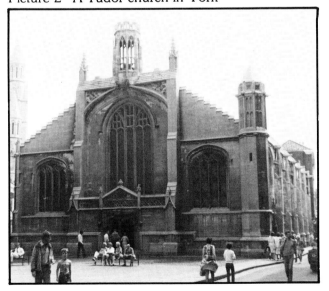

Picture 3   A Catholic church

A Protestant church

The local church was not just a place for worshipping God. Very important information was kept there too. In 1538 Henry VIII's chief adviser Thomas Cromwell ordered the priests *'to keep one book or register for every church. In it you shall write the day and year of every wedding, christening and burying made in your parish while you are there. Each priest that comes after you must do the same'.*

We can look at lots of these parish registers today. They tell us many useful and interesting things about Tudor people.

☆ ☆ ☆ TO DO ☆ ☆ ☆

1. Look at the Catholic church in Picture 3. Then list all the things that are different in the Protestant church. Which one do you prefer? Say why.

2. Make up a conversation between a Tudor Puritan and someone who is always misbehaving in church. Get them to talk about: sermons; reading the Bible; what the church looks like inside; holy water; people who stay away from church; the parish register; the churchwarden.

10 VILLAGE LIFE

Picture 1 is a painting from Tudor times. It shows villagers getting in the hay. That year, the harvest had been good. But every 5 or 6 years, bad weather spoiled the crops, and some people starved to death. So every Spring, in 'Rogation week', the villagers prayed for fine weather.

They marched right around the parish, behind the local priest. At special places, there were sermons, psalm-singing and prayers for a good harvest. The villagers ate, drank and played around a lot on these days. They were called 'gang days' or 'cross days'.

There were special holy days all through the year. They helped people to remember what they had to do. One book on farming said:

Plant your garlic and beans on St Edmund's Day, and finish sowing your wheat by Hallowmas Eve.

People were not supposed to eat meat during Lent. They often paid their rent on Lady Day, and thought it was unlucky to put shoes on horses on St Loy's Day.

Picture 1

Picture 2 At Great Gransdon in Huntingdonshire, the villagers had a strange Rogation custom. They held the priest upside down, with his head in a water-hole!

Most people lived in villages, not in towns. The villagers all worked, played and prayed together. They got to know one another very well. A German visitor wrote in 1602:

In England, everyone has to keep a sharp eye on his neighbour's home, to check if the married people are getting on well together.

Villagers were expected to spy on each other, and report people who were breaking the law. In those days, there were no policemen like ours. But most villages had a sort of detective. This was the local 'cunning man' or 'cunning woman'.

These people were not like modern detectives at all. They also used magic to cure diseases, and told the villagers' fortunes. One of the ways that a cunning man might solve a crime was to take some pieces of paper. On them he would write the names of all the people who were *suspected*. Then he would wrap them in little clay balls, and put them in a bucket of water. The one that came unrolled first had the name of the guilty person on it!

Picture 3   This poor man could not find work in the countryside. So he went to the town. He could look for a job or beg there.

☆☆☆ TO DO ☆☆☆

1. What things would you have liked about being a Tudor villager? What things would you not have liked? Make two lists.

2. What jobs did cunning men and women do? Why do we not have people like them today?

23

11 TOWNS AND CITIES

Picture 1 London Bridge, just after Queen Elizabeth died.

In 1564, the people of Chelmsford in Essex were told to obey these local laws:

First, every inhabitant of the town must scour and make clean the gutter which goes through the town, once in every month. Otherwise he must pay one shilling.

Also, neither the butcher nor anyone else must throw horns, bones or any other filth into the street or river. Fine for doing so, three shillings and fourpence.

Also, no inhabitant of any house must kill any cattle or anything else in his house, which might annoy his neighbours. Fine for doing so, twenty shillings.

There were no dustmen in Tudor towns.

Houses had no running water, and were often packed close together. When someone caught a disease from the filth, it soon spread along the street. Fires spread quickly too, because the shops and houses were mainly made of wood. You can see lots of wooden buildings on London Bridge in Picture 1.

London was the biggest city in England. It was also one of the biggest in the world. Visitors thought it was terribly busy. Thomas Dekker wrote in 1606:

In every street carts and coaches make such a thundering. At every corner men, women and children meet in such crowds, that posts are set up to strengthen the houses, in case the people should

Picture 2 Two busy men in Tudor London: the cutpurse, who stole people's things in the crowded streets; the water-carrier, who went from door to door, selling water for washing and drinking.

shoulder them down as they jostle one another. Besides, hammers are beating in one place, tubs hooping in another, pots clinking in a third. Here are porters sweating under heavy loads. There are merchants' men carrying bags of money.

Picture 3 This inn at Holborn is one of the few Tudor buildings still standing in London .

By the end of Tudor times, about 200 000 people lived in London. This list from 1588 shows what sort of jobs they did, and how much they were paid each year. As well as the money, they were given food and drink:

Clothworkers	£5
Dyers	£6 13s 4d
Shoemakers	£4
Whitebakers	£4 13s 4d
Brewers	£10
The miller	£6
Saddlers	£4
Blacksmiths	£6
Brownbakers	£3 6s 8d
Glovers	£3 6s 8d
Cappers	£4 13s 4d
Butchers	£6

☆ ☆ ☆ TO DO ☆ ☆ ☆

1. **a)** Say what jobs the workers in the list above did. **b)** Which workers in the list were paid the most? **c)** Which workers were paid the least?

2. Many shoppers could not read. So butchers, for example, put pictures of meat on signs outside their shops. These signs showed shoppers what they could buy inside. Draw signs for all the other workers in the list.

3. Write about a day-trip to London around 1600. Mention: cutpurses; water-carriers; traffic; crowds; smells; shops; London Bridge.

12 FOREIGN VISITORS

Picture 1   These were the most important places in Europe in 1559.

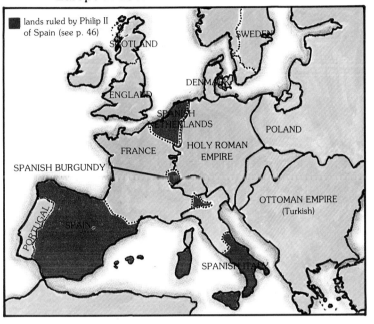

lands ruled by Philip II of Spain (see p. 46)

SCOTLAND
SWEDEN
DENMARK
ENGLAND
SPANISH NETHERLANDS
POLAND
FRANCE
HOLY ROMAN EMPIRE
SPANISH BURGUNDY
PORTUGAL
SPAIN
OTTOMAN EMPIRE (Turkish)
SPANISH ITALY

Have you ever been to a foreign country? In Tudor times, most people did not travel abroad very much. But some foreigners *did* visit England. Sometimes they wrote down things about English people and customs. We can read their reports today. They tell us a lot about life in Tudor England.

In 1499, a Dutchman called Erasmus wrote:

Wherever you come in England, everyone kisses you; when you go away, everyone kisses you again; when you come back, more kisses. In short, wherever you move there is nothing but kisses.

But a German duke thought English people were very unfriendly. He wrote in 1592:

The people of London care little for foreigners, but laugh at them. You dare not argue with them, or else the street-boys collect together in huge crowds and strike at you without mercy.

In 1551, an Italian visitor wrote about children too:

The English keep their children at home till they are 7 or 9 at the most. Then they send both boys and girls to go and work in the houses of other people. They usually have to do this for another 7 or 9 years. The children are called apprentices, and they have to do all the nastiest jobs.

Then in 1598, a German traveller wrote:

The English are vastly fond of great noises that fill the ear, such as the firing of cannon, drums, and the ringing of bells.

It is usual for a number of them to get drunk, then go into some bell-tower, and ring the bells for hours on end, just for exercise.

The German also wrote:

If they see a handsome foreigner, they will say, It is a pity he is not an Englishman!

Picture 2 The 'Evil May Day' riot in London. On 1 May 1517, gangs of apprentices attack and kill foreign merchants in the city.

Picture 3 Foreigners were often asked to come to England, to do special jobs. A Frenchman made this 'astronomical clock' for Henry VIII at Hampton Court. It was sometimes called 'the Clock of Death' — it was supposed to stop whenever anyone died in the palace.

✮ ✮ ✮ TO DO ✮ ✮ ✮

1. Pretend you are a 9-year-old in Tudor times. What would you like about living with another family? What would you dislike? Say what it would be like to live with:

a) a rich family;

b) a poor family. (To help you, look at pages 32-3.)

2. Look at the map of Europe in 1559. Then look at a map of Europe today.

a) List all the countries which are on both maps.

b) List all the countries which are on the 1559 map but not on the modern map.

c) List all the countries that were ruled by Philip II.

d) Which countries have taken the place of the Holy Roman Empire and the Ottoman Empire today?

13 STRANGE CURES

Picture 1 The surgery of Dr John Hall in Stratford-upon-Avon. It is part of a Tudor house that is now a museum.

Most Tudor people did not keep clean and healthy. They were not so 'hygienic' as we are today. This was one reason why they caught lots of terrible diseases. Doctors did not know how to cure many of them. Some doctors told their patients to swallow powdered human skull, or buttered live spiders!

To cure a disease called 'consumption' they were told to:

take a sow pig of 9 days old and put her in a stillory (tank) with a handful of spearmint, half a handful of turnip, a handful of celery, 9 dates and two crushed sticks of good cinnamon. Put this over a fair fire and get the juice out of it. Then put the juice in a glass, and stand it in the sun for 9 days, then drink 9 spoonfuls of it at once.

Only rich people could afford to pay doctors. Poor people had to make up their own medicines, or else they asked the local cunning man or woman to help them (see page 23). One of their ways to cure toothache was for the patient to write these words three times on a piece of paper:

Jesus Christ for mercy sake
Take away this toothache.

Then he had to say it out loud, and burn the paper. The next time you have toothache, try it!

In 1585, some English explorers in America found a strange plant. They thought it was a wonderful new medicine. One of them wrote:

Sailors and all others who come back from America use little funnels made of palm leaves or straw. They stuff crumbled dried leaves of this plant in the end of the funnel. They light this, and

Picture 2 This is a Tudor painting of Queen Mary I, trying to cure a sick person. Many people believed that kings and queens could cure a disease called scrofula, just by touching the infected skin. All the Tudor rulers tried to cure people in this way.

opening their mouths as much as they can, they suck in the smoke with their breath. They say this cures their hunger and thirst, sores, wounds and plague-fever.

What was the name of this plant? People soon found out that it was *not* a medicine. Sir Thomas Hariot was one of the explorers in America. He was probably the first Englishman to get lung cancer from smoking and die.

Picture 3 These things were found on board the *Mary Rose*. They were part of a barber-surgeon's kit. (Barber-surgeons cut hair, pulled out teeth and did small operations on people. In Tudor times, there were no hospitals like ours.) Someone found a wooden mallet with these things on the *Mary Rose*. Perhaps it was for knocking patients out before operations!

☆ ☆ ☆ **TO DO** ☆ ☆ ☆

1. How is the surgery in Picture 1
a) different from your doctor's surgery;
b) the same as your doctor's surgery?

2. Draw a picture of a barber-surgeon using the things in Picture 3.
Clue – think first about what jobs he might have to do on board a warship.

3. a) What is the man behind Queen Mary in Picture 2 doing?
b) Why do you think people believed kings and queens could cure scrofula?
c) Do you think this cure ever worked? Say why or why not.

14 CHIMNEYS EVERYWHERE!

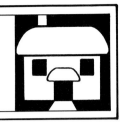

Picture 1

Do you live in a house with an upstairs and a downstairs? If you do not, do you know someone else's house like that? Now imagine that the stairs in it are gone. Imagine that the downstairs ceiling is gone. In early Tudor times, big houses had no upstairs and downstairs, but they had very high ceilings.

Imagine that there is a big open fire in the middle of the main room. The smoke makes the inside walls all sooty, and goes out through a hole in the roof. Sometimes, the wind blows the smoke back in. In the winter, everyone in the house huddles around the fire together, to keep warm. People do not have their own rooms.

Now look at Picture 1. It shows some beautiful brick chimneys at Hampton Court palace. More and more Tudor people started putting chimney-stacks into their houses. In 1577, some old men talked to William Harrison about:

the great many chimneys put up lately. In their young days, there were not more than two or three in most towns of the realm, except for the monasteries and perhaps the manor houses of some great noblemen.

These chimneys made a lot of difference to people's houses. Picture 2 shows you a rich person's house, without its front wall. You can see that there are quite a few small rooms in it. The rooms had their own fireplaces, and the smoke from them went up the new chimneys. The family and servants no longer had to mix together around the fire in a big main hall. Picture 3 shows what one of the upstairs bedrooms might have looked like. The bedroom is in a Tudor house near Stratford, that is still standing today.

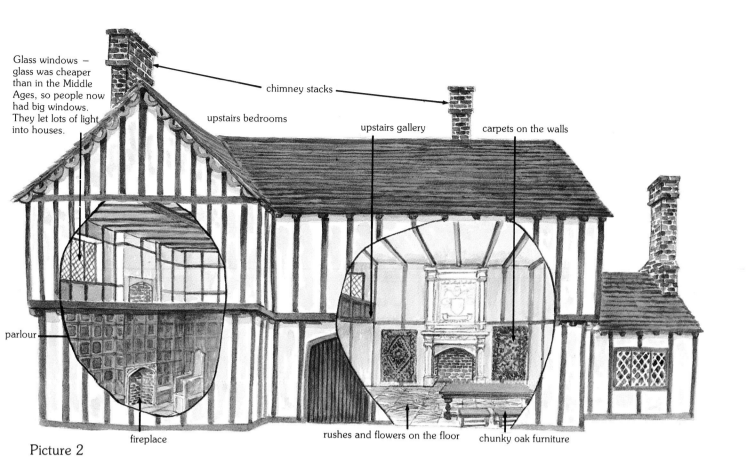

Glass windows – glass was cheaper than in the Middle Ages, so people now had big windows. They let lots of light into houses.

chimney stacks

upstairs bedrooms

upstairs gallery

carpets on the walls

parlour

fireplace

rushes and flowers on the floor

chunky oak furniture

Picture 2

Picture 3 A bedroom in Anne Hathaway's cottage, near Stratford-upon-Avon.

Anne Hathaway was quite a rich person. But even her cottage had no running water, no bathroom, no indoor toilet, no electric light, few soft chairs with backs or arms, and no carpets on the floors. Poor people's homes had hardly *any* furniture in them. Sometimes the people lived under the same roof as their pigs and cows. But it is hard for us to know just what these dark, cramped houses were like. Nearly all of them have fallen down, burned down or been knocked down.

☆☆☆ TO DO ☆☆☆

1. Why did lots of Tudor people put chimney-stacks in their houses? Why were Tudor people keen to have glass in their windows?

2. When you visit a Tudor house nowadays, why was it probably a rich person's house?

3. Look at the bedroom in Picture 3. Is it different from your parents' bedroom? Make lists of the things in both bedrooms. Which one do you prefer? Say why.

Picture 1 A brass picture of the Forde family, which was put up in a Tudor church.

Picture 1 shows a big Tudor family. But lots of children died of diseases before they grew up. Those who lived were treated very harshly. One book about bringing up children said that *'a youth is just an untamed beast.'* Most parents believed that they had to tame these young beasts. Teachers believed the same thing too. *'I have strange news brought me this morning,'* wrote William Cecil, Elizabeth I's chief minister, in 1563, *'that many schoolboys at Eton have run away from the school for fear of being beaten.'*

Teachers might give naughty pupils 50 strokes of the birch, a type of cane, in one day; or they might hit them across the mouth with a 'ferula', a flat piece of wood with a hole in it. At Westminster School, teachers had to pick *'monitors from among the most serious schoolboys, to watch the behaviour of the rest everywhere and stop anything dirty being done. If any monitor does not do his duty properly he shall be flogged hard as an example to others.'*

Only rich boys went to schools like Eton and Westminster. In Tudor times, children did not *have* to go to school. Poor parents made their children go to work as soon as they were old enough. Often they became servants and apprentices, and went to live in their masters' houses (see page 26). Most girls, rich or poor, never went to school at all. Their parents just wanted them to be good wives one day. So they spent most of their time learning how to do housework.

A girl's parents often chose her husband for her. Boys had more chance of making

Picture 2 A Tudor teacher and his pupils.

up their own minds. But William Cecil told *his* son Robert:

to take great care in choosing a wife, for she will be the cause of all the good or bad that happens to you in the future . . . Do not choose a dwarf or a fool, for from the first you may have pygmy children, and from the second you will find to your grief that there is nothing more horrible than a she-fool.

Tudor weddings were different from our

Picture 3 This picture from Tudor times shows a husband beating his wife. The children are watching close by.

weddings today. Poor girls could not afford wedding dresses; and even rich girls did not wear white. *'The bride was dressed in a russet* (reddish-brown) *woollen gown,'* wrote Thomas Delony at one Tudor wedding, *'and a kertle* (petti-coat on the outside) *of fine wool. Her hair, as yellow as gold, hung down behind her.'* As soon as a girl was married, she plaited her long hair, and wore it under a hood or cap.

The life of a wife could be very hard. Lots of Tudor men treated their brides as if *they were untamed beasts.* In Gloucestershire there was a saying, *'A woman, a spaniel, a walnut tree, the more they are beaten, the better they be.'* Nowadays, things are much fairer. Girls and women are treated in the same way as boys and men.

☆ ☆ ☆ TO DO ☆ ☆ ☆

1. Look at Picture 1.
a) How many people are in the Forde family?
b) Describe what the man and his wife are wearing.
c) What books do you think are open in front of them? Why do you think this?

2. Describe all the things that are happening in Picture 2. Do you think that the teacher is in control of his pupils? Say why.

3. Would you rather have been a boy or a girl in Tudor times? Explain why.

16 FANCY DRESS

In 1981, the wreck of the *Mary Rose* was still on the seabed. A man dived down to explore it. 'I was down there one day,' he said, 'working on a gun-carriage. Suddenly I found that I was not alone. Lying almost next to me was the skeleton of a man. He was still wearing his leather jacket and his leather shoes. Everything else had gone.'

The mud had stopped these Tudor clothes from rotting away. They help us to know what ordinary people used to wear. But most other Tudor clothes *have* rotted away. So we have to look at Tudor pictures, and read Tudor descriptions, to find out what people wore.

William Powncett was a merchant in London. These clothes belonged to him in 1553:

an old cloth gown faced with damask (silk weaving)	10s 0d
an old coat of black velvet striped with lace	33s 4d
a torn velvet doublet	20s 0d
a jacket of black velvet	33s 4d
a red mantle (cloak)	4s 0d
a gown lined with squirrel skins and faced with martens (small animals like weasels)	60s 0d

These things were very fine and expensive. Poorer people had to make do with home-made clothes in cheap materials. Sometimes they had only one set of clothes, and they had to wear these clothes until they fell to pieces.

Picture 1

Picture 2 A beautiful Tudor jewel. Philip Stubbes thought that men and women wore far too much jewellery: *'They must have their looking-glasses with them wheresoever they go; and for good reason, for how else could they see the devil in them?'*

Many people certainly were keen to look their best in public. A German visitor wrote in 1599, *'I have been told that quite a few English women wear velvet on the street but cannot afford a crust of dry bread at home.'*

Artists did not paint many pictures of poor people (but you can see one on page 23). They painted many more pictures of rich people, who could afford to pay them for the paintings. Picture 1 shows guests at a wedding in 1590. People usually wear their best clothes at weddings, or when they are having their pictures painted. The wedding-guests in the picture probably wore much simpler clothes at home.

You can see how popular hats were. In 1583, Philip Stubbes wrote that men's hats sometimes looked like *'steeples, standing a quarter of a yard above the crown of their heads.'* Starched collars called 'ruffs' were also in fashion. Men's ruffs could be more than a foot wide, and then, wrote Stubbes, *'they go flip-flap in the wind and lie upon their shoulders like a dishcloth.'*

Some of the women are wearing cutaway dresses, to show off the fine material underneath. Stubbes thought that some women wore so many layers of clothes that they *'seemed not women of flesh and blood, but rather puppets made up of rags and patches.'* Their skirts stand out, because the women are wearing frames underneath called farthingales, fixed to their waists.

One or two of the women might be wearing wigs.

They are not content with their own hair, but buy other hair, wrote Stubbes, *either of horses, mares or any other strange beasts, and dye it. I heard of one who met a little child with very fair hair, invited her into a house, promised her a penny, and so cut off her hair.*

☆ ☆ ☆ TO DO ☆ ☆ ☆

1. a) Describe all the different types of hat people are wearing in Picture 1. **b)** Choose *one* of the people in Picture 1, and say what it *felt* like to be wearing his or her clothes.

2. Why do Tudor pictures not tell us *exactly* what people used to wear? Can you think of any other ways that we might find out about Tudor clothes? What do you think Philip Stubbes would say about the clothes *you* wear today? (Would he think you dress simply, and without too much decoration?)

Picture 1   A Tudor painting of Lord Cobham and his family. They are just finishing off a meal. Describe all the things on the table. What was *unhygienic* about this meal?

Write down what times you had your meals last Friday. Then list everything you ate and drank. Did you eat any meat? In Tudor times, you were not *allowed* to eat meat on Fridays, or during Lent. This was a religious rule. But people were allowed to eat fish on those days. So the rule helped fishermen to sell lots of their fish.

Rich families, like the Cobhams in Picture 1, had very interesting meals. The menu opposite shows what they *might* have

eaten on a Friday. They took their pick from all the things on the table. Children and grown-ups ate and drank all the same things — even the beer and wine!

On other days of the week, rich people ate all sorts of meat. William Harrison wrote:

They have not only beef, mutton, veal, lamb, kid, pork, cony (rabbit), capon, pig, but also some portion of the red or fallow deer beside great variety of wild birds.

36

7 a.m. Breakfast — Bean porridge, salted fish, bread — Beer

Salad of home-grown lettuce, radishes, cucumber, onions

12 a.m. Dinner — Salmon soaked in vinegar, served with sour sauce — Home-brewed beer, cider, wine from Gascony in France

Eel roasted in a sheet of paper, with oil, coriander and parsley

Lobster, crayfish, shrimps, oysters

A plate of fruit, nuts, home-made cheese

6 p.m. Supper — Fried carp sprinkled with spiced vinegar — Mulled wine (hot wine with sugar and spices in it)

Plates of sole, turbot and pike

Almond biscuits

They often caught diseases because they did not eat many fresh vegetables, or drink much milk. Their teeth usually went black too. This was because they ate lots of sweet things, but did not clean their teeth properly afterwards.

Poorer people had to make do with vegetable stews and bread. They could not afford much meat. William Harrison wrote that when times were hard, *'they may have to content themselves with bread made of beans, peas or oats or of all together and some acorns too'.* Neither rich people nor poor people had healthy diets. Make a list of all the things you eat and drink today that are good for you.

Picture 2   This kitchen is in a Tudor house near Stratford. There was no oven. Food was boiled in a cauldron (large pot) over the fire, or roasted on spits. There was no fridge to keep meat fresh in. Sometimes it went bad. People then cooked it in hot spices, to hide the horrible taste.

Manners

Children had to be on their best behaviour at mealtimes. These rules are in a book from 1577:

Scratche not thy head with thy fingers when thou arte at thy meate;
Pick not thy teeth with thy knife nor with thy fingers ende;
Fyll not thy mouth too full, lest thou perhaps must speak;
Nor blow not out thy crums when thou dost eate.
Foule not the place with spitting where thou doest sit.

Put these rules into modern English words. Remember – 'thou' means 'you' and 'thy' means 'your'.

SPORTS AND GAMES

Look at Picture 1. What do you think it is? The German Emperor gave it to Henry VIII as a present. It was a special helmet for jousting. In Picture 2, you can see Henry jousting at Westminster, in front of Queen Katherine and her ladies.

There were lots of games and shows to enjoy at court. In 1579, Queen Elizabeth paid £6 13s 4d to Lord Stanley's acrobats. This was for *'certain feats of tumbling done by them before Her Majesty upon Tuesday the 15th of January'*. Elizabeth must have been pleased with the acrobats – she paid them an extra £3 6s 8d as well.

Rich people had plenty of time to joust, watch shows, hunt and dance. Poorer people had less free time. But they still enjoyed many pastimes, especially on feast days and holy days (see page 22). Football, wrestling, bowls, skittles and cards were all popular games to play. Picture 4 shows some things found on the *Mary Rose*. We can look at them, and work out how ordinary sailors spent *their* free time.

Men and women enjoyed playing games and drinking in public houses. In those days, there were no laws to stop children from going into public houses too. But there *were* laws that said all men should

Picture 1

practise shooting with bows and arrows. This was because they might have to fight in a war. Archers were still very important in battles. They could fire at enemies who were 300 metres away.

Picture 2

Picture 3 Dancing courtiers

Hugh Latimer was a boy in early Tudor times. He wrote that his father taught him *'how to draw, how to lay my body into the bow. I had my bows brought to me according to my age and strength; as I increased in them, so my bows were made bigger and bigger. For men shall never shoot well unless they be brought up to it.'*

Yet men had to be careful. In Mary's reign, an archer was arrested because he shot his arrows *too* well. People believed that he used witchcraft to help him!

Picture 4 Things found on the 'Mary Rose': a wooden board, for playing backgammon; the specially-sharpened leg-spur of a gaming cock (these birds were made to fight one another, while spectators betted on who would win); a wind instrument like a recorder.

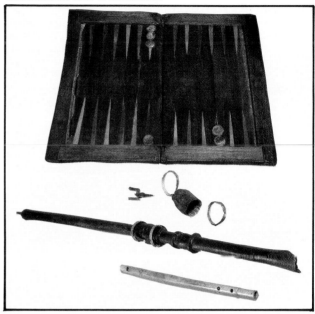

☆ ☆ ☆ **TO DO** ☆ ☆ ☆

1.   a) Name three ways of finding out how people enjoyed themselves in Tudor times.

b) How much did Queen Elizabeth pay the acrobats altogether? (Check up on how pounds, shillings and pence worked on page 15.)

2.   a) Name the instruments that the musicians are playing in Picture 3.

b) Pretend you are a sailor on board the *Mary Rose*. Tell a friend back at home how you spend your free time.

3. Where do you think men practised with their bows and arrows? Draw a picture of a practice session. Show some young boys practising too.

Picture 1   1 A flag with a swan on it. This showed people that there was a play on that afternoon. Plays had to be in the afternoons. There was no way of lighting up the theatre in the evenings.

2 The theatre has an open roof, like a football ground today.

3 People watching in a covered area or 'gallery'.

4 The actors on the big stage. Usually men played the women's parts too.

5 There is no scenery.

6 Places for people to watch from. People also watched from the ground in front of the stage.

In 1597, the Lord Mayor of London wrote, *Theatres are the meeting places for thieves, horse-stealers and other idle and dangerous persons. They draw apprentices and other servants from their work. All sorts of people go to theatres instead of listening to sermons. In time of sickness, many ill people go to hear a play, and give their diseases to others* .

In 1590, a Dutchman called de Witt visited London. He wrote:

There are four theatres of great beauty. In each of them a different play is shown to the people every day. Of all the theatres, the largest and the most magnificent is the one called the Swan Theatre; 3 000 people can sit there.

Picture 1 shows de Witt's drawing of the *Swan* Theatre. His writing is in Latin. We have added the words in English.

Both rich and poor people enjoyed watching plays. The cartoon strip on page 41 shows you the story of one of these plays. It was called *Romeo and Juliet*. William Shakespeare, a great Tudor playwright, wrote it. You can still see his plays at the theatre or on television. They help us to find out how Tudor people talked, thought and lived.

☆☆☆ TO DO ☆☆☆

1. Look at Picture 1. There are two sets of doors at the back of the stage. What do you think they were for?

2. Pretend you are living in Shakespeare's time. You are sitting in the covered gallery of the *Swan*, watching *Romeo and Juliet*. Draw a picture of any part of the play, showing what you can see.

2 Juliet's cousin picks a quarrel with Romeo. They have a sword fight, and Romeo kills him. The Prince of Verona is furious. He orders Romeo to leave Verona forever.

1 Romeo and Juliet live in Verona in Italy. They meet at a party and fall in love. A friendly Friar marries them in secret. They do not dare to tell their parents as the two families hate each other.

3 Juliet is terribly sad. She then hears her parents have chosen a young nobleman to be her husband. But she is already secretly married – to Romeo. In despair she asks the Friar for help.

4 The Friar gives her a strange mixture to drink. It will make her sleep very, very deeply for nearly two days. Her parents will think she is dead and put her in the family tomb. Meanwhile, the Friar will write to Romeo and explain about the mixture. He will also ask Romeo to come and take Juliet away from the tomb when she wakes up.

6 Romeo is so sad that he poisons himself. Then Juliet wakes up. She sees Romeo's body and is heartbroken. So she seizes his dagger and kills herself too. When the two families find out, they swear never to quarrel again.

5 Juliet drinks the mixture. Her heartbroken parents think she is dead, and put her in the tomb. But Romeo does not get the Friar's letter! Instead someone tells him that Juliet is really dead. He rushes back to Verona and finds Juliet in the tomb. She is still asleep but Romeo believes she is dead.

41

Picture 1 ▼
Princess Elizabeth was born in 1533 (see page 9). She was a clever and lively girl. An Italian visitor said that she was *'tall and well formed, with a good skin; she has fine eyes and above all beautiful hands which she likes to show off.'* The princess grew up in dangerous times. In 1536, her mother was executed. In 1557, her half-sister Mary shut her up in the Tower of London. Mary believed that Elizabeth was plotting against her.

Picture 3 ▲
Elizabeth worked very hard at ruling England. She travelled around often, so that her people could see her. They called her 'Good Queen Bess', 'Gloriana' and 'The Fairy Queen'. But her advisers knew that she had a bad temper too. One of them wrote, *'When she smiled it was pure sunshine, but soon a storm came and thunder fell on everyone!'*

Picture 2 ►
Elizabeth's coronation. In 1558 Mary died and Elizabeth became queen. She was only 25 years old. Everyone expected her to marry. Then she could have children, who could rule England after she died. But Elizabeth never married. She once said, *'I will have here just one mistress and no master!'*

Picture 4 ▲
A 'miniature' of Elizabeth, painted in 1572. Her people wore tiny portraits like these close to their hearts, or even on their hats or shoe-buckles.

Picture 6 ▲
Elizabeth in old age. A German visitor saw Elizabeth at the end of her life. He wrote that *'her teeth are very yellow and unequal. Many of them are missing, so that you cannot understand her easily when she speaks quickly.'* But she kept on working hard — and losing her temper! When she was very ill, her chief adviser told her she must rest. She spat at him, *'Little man, you do not use the word* **must** *when you talk to queens!'* She died at last in 1603.

Picture 5 ▲
In 1588, the English navy defeated the Spanish Armada (see pages 46-7). Afterwards Elizabeth told her people, *'I know I have the body of a weak and feeble woman, but I have the heart of a king, and of a king of England too.'* She then had this picture painted of herself. She was more than 50 years old, but the painter made her look much younger. Elizabeth did not want her people to think she looked old.

☆ ☆ ☆ **TO DO** ☆ ☆ ☆

a) Why do some paintings of Elizabeth not show *exactly* what she looked like?

b) Why did Elizabeth want her people to think she always looked young?

c) Why did Elizabeth dress in such gorgeous clothes in her paintings?

d) Why are there ships in Picture 5 and a skeleton in Picture 6?

e) Do you think Elizabeth looked more like her grandfather or her father? (You can find their pictures on pages 7 and 9.) Say why.

21 | ROUND THE WORLD

Picture 1

Look at Picture 1. It shows a model of a Tudor ship, the *Golden Hind*. This ship was much smaller than the *Mary Rose* (see pages 4 and 5). It was only about 30 metres long, and 6 metres wide. But it was the first English ship to sail right round the world!

The captain of the *Golden Hind* was Francis Drake. Queen Elizabeth wanted him to explore unknown lands in South America. She also wanted him to bring back gold and silver. But the Spaniards had already conquered many parts of South America. So Drake's men had to fight the Spaniards to get the treasure. Picture 3 shows you what happened on the long voyage.

In April 1579, a captured Spanish captain met Drake on board the *Golden Hind*. He wrote:

Drake is served on silver dishes with gold borders, on which are his coat of arms. He carries perfumed waters and all sorts of dainty things with him. He dines and sups to the music of viols. He also has painters on board. They paint for him pictures of the coast in its exact colours.

Other Spaniards called Drake 'the Dragon'. They believed that he had a magic mirror. It was supposed to show him where Spanish treasure ships were, so that he could seize them!

At last Drake got home safely. The Queen was very glad. She brought the *Golden Hind* to London. In front of cheering crowds, she made Drake a knight. The 'master-pirate' was now *Sir Francis Drake*.

Picture 2 Sir Francis Drake

✯ ✯ ✯ TO DO ✯ ✯ ✯

1. Trace the map. Then work out where the *Golden Hind* was, when the Spaniard went aboard. Mark the spot on the map, and draw a picture of the *Golden Hind* next to it.

2. Pretend you are one of Drake's sailors. Write a diary of the things that happen on the voyage. Remember to mention: the visit of the Spaniard; life on board the little ship; homesickness; what Drake looked like.

Picture 3   Major points of Drake's voyage around world

1. 13 Dec 1577 Drake's ships leave Plymouth

2. 18 June 1578 An officer, Doughty, tries to get some sailors to disobey Drake. Drake puts him on trial and executes him

3. Sept 1578 Only the *Golden Hind* sails on from here

4. 5 Dec 1578 Drake seizes 25 000 pesos of gold from a Spanish ship. Then he goes on seizing treasure up the coast

5. 1 March 1579 Drake captures a great Spanish treasure-ship the *Cacafuego*

6. July 1579 Drake declares that New Albion belongs to Queen Elizabeth. (This land is now called California)

7. Aug 1579 Drake cannot find a way to sail home around the top of North America. So he heads home across the Pacific Ocean

8. 9 Feb 1580 The *Golden Hind* is almost wrecked on a reef (rocks under the water)

9. 26 Sept 1580 The *Golden Hind* returns to Plymouth

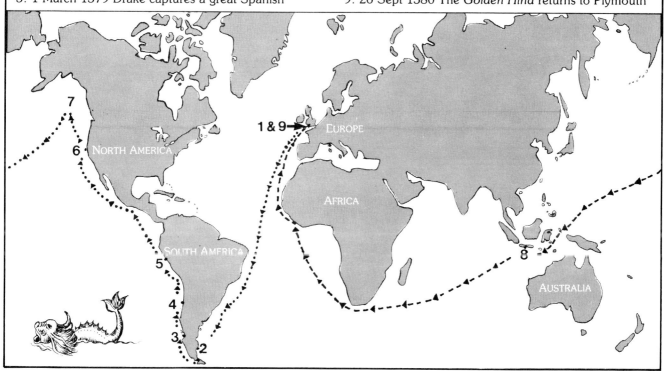

Picture 1 Philip II and his wife Queen Mary Tudor

Picture 2 The Armada outside Calais

It was August, 1588. The Spaniards were coming! They planned to invade England, and make it a Catholic country again. Their king, Philip II, wanted to be king of England too. Thirty years before, he *had* been king of England. That was when he was married to Queen Mary Tudor. You can *see* them together in Picture 1. But Philip and Queen Elizabeth had argued. Spain and England had been at war since 1585.

Elizabeth waited at court. She knew that a huge fleet, the Armada, had left Spain. There were 130 ships in it. Each ship was packed with the best soldiers in Europe. Elizabeth knew that the Armada *had* to be stopped, before those soldiers could land. She was relying on Sir Francis Drake and her other sea-captains. Only they could stop the great Armada.

Suddenly news came from Plymouth. The Armada had been seen in the English Channel!

Robert Carey was at court at that moment. Later, he wrote down what happened:

Lord Cumberland and I rode straight to Portsmouth. There we found a small ship that carried us to sea. On the Thursday we joined the English fleet. All that day we followed close the Spanish Armada.

We did the same on Friday and Saturday. Then the Armada cast anchor just outside Calais. We did the same, a very small distance behind them.

Then our commanders got six old ships, and stuffed them full of things that would burn. On Monday at two in the morning they were let loose. Each ship had a man aboard to direct her. The tide took them very near the Armada. Then the men set fire to their own ships, and came away in little boats. The burning ships headed straight for the Armada.

The Spaniards had to try to escape in haste. They got into great disorder. We prepared to follow them. There began a cruel fight. The wind and the tide helped us to defeat them. The fight lasted from 4 o'clock in the morning till almost 5 or 6 at night. They lost a dozen or fourteen of their best ships. God had given us this great victory. The Spaniards made all haste to get away.

Picture 4 shows where they went. Only about half the Armada got back to Spain. Philip II's plans had failed. England stayed a Protestant country; and Elizabeth carried on being queen until she died, in 1603. To find out what happened after that, you must read THE STUARTS AND GEORGIANS.

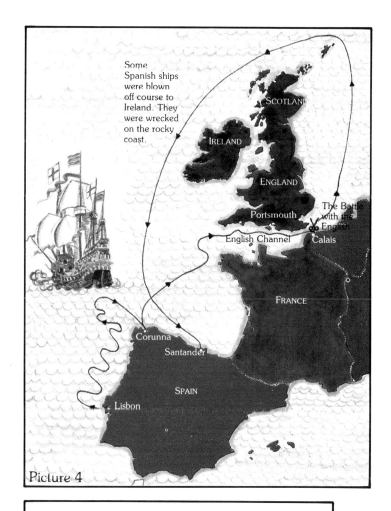

Picture 4

Some Spanish ships were blown off course to Ireland. They were wrecked on the rocky coast.

SCOTLAND

IRELAND

ENGLAND

Portsmouth

The Battle with the English

English Channel

Calais

FRANCE

Corunna

Santander

SPAIN

Lisbon

Picture 3 A Tudor medal showing what happened to the Armada on its way home.

☆☆☆ TO DO ☆☆☆

1. Read pages 44-5 ('Round the World') again, and give one reason why you think England and Spain went to war.

2. a) What parts of the Armada story do Pictures 2 and 3 show?
b) Look at Picture 4. Why did the Armada sail home around the *top* of Britain?

3. Pretend you are Philip II. What orders do you give the Armada, before it sets sail? What do you tell the soldiers to do, once they have landed in England? Explain to them why they must conquer England, and tell them to fight their hardest.

HOW TO BE A HISTORIAN

First of all, get yourself a pocket notebook. Take it with you when you visit museums, historical places and libraries. Jot down important information on Tudor Times in it, and draw anything that looks interesting.

You will then need a big scrapbook or exercise book. When you get home from each visit, start a new page, put the date at the top, and write down carefully everything you saw and did. Look at the notes in your notebook to remind yourself. You could copy some of your drawings into the book.

Historians need to keep a 'record' or diary like this. It stops them from forgetting things; and it is useful to have all their information in one place. Write on the cover of your scrapbook

Tudor Times
A Record kept by (your name)

Here are some ways of finding information to put in your Record:

VISITING MUSEUMS

Always remember to
● decide what you want to look for in the museum before you visit it. For example, you might want to look at Tudor armour, or household objects. Usually, there are so many things in museums that it is impossible to look at *everything* properly.
● check if there are any leaflets or museum guides on sale. These will help you to find your way around and explain some of the things on show.
● check if you can find any postcards of the things on show. They would be useful to stick in your Record.

If you can, try to visit Stratford-on-Avon. You can go round several Tudor houses there that have been turned into museums.

VISITING HISTORICAL PLACES

(like Hampton Court, Fountains Abbey and the other places you have read about in this book)

Always remember to
● go first to the shop where they sell leaflets and guides. You will probably be able to buy postcards and maps for your Record there too.
● try hard to imagine what the place *used* to look like. In your notebook, do a drawing of how it looks today; then do another one, showing how you *think* it looked in Tudor Times. Put people and animals in this second drawing.

WATCHING, LISTENING AND READING

People are always discovering new things about Tudor Times. Watch out for television and radio programmes about these discoveries. You can find out more about them in newspapers, which you can read in public libraries. Picture 1 shows the front page of *The Daily Mirror*, on the day after the 'Mary Rose' (see page 4) was lifted off the seabed. Libraries also have lots of books on

Picture 1